STUDY GUIDE

Jonathan Edwards

Stephen J. Nichols

I0806866

LIGONIER MINISTRIES
Renew your Mind.
LIGONIER.ORG | 800-435-4343

Copyright © 2012 Ligonier Ministries
421 Ligonier Court, Sanford, FL 32771
E-mail: info@ligonier.org
All rights reserved.
No reproduction of this work without permission.
Printed in the United States of America.

1

His Early Life

MESSAGE INTRODUCTION

Human beings tend to romanticize and idealize the lives of those individuals we admire, particularly those that lived in an era far removed from ourselves. We smooth out a wrinkle here, turn a blind eye to an episode there, and, poof, an impeccable figure emerges from a charmed existence. The great American theologian Jonathan Edwards has not escaped this idealizing. Yet, a full understanding of his theology and the decisions he made demands a realistic examination of his life, from beginning to end. Dr. Steve Nichols takes us through the life of Edwards in this study, illuminating the details of his life, good and bad, so that we might better understand how God cultivated and crafted Edwards into His servant—who many consider the greatest theologian the United States has ever produced.

TEACHING OBJECTIVES

1. To examine influential elements of the early life of Edwards
2. To demonstrate how Edwards began to form intentionality in his life
3. To introduce Edwards' desire to learn two books: the Bible and the book of nature

QUOTATION

God's purpose for my life was that I have a passion for God's glory and that I have a passion for my joy in that glory, and that these two are one passion.

—Jonathan Edwards

LECTURE OUTLINE

I. The Early Life of Jonathan Edwards
   A. Edwards was born to Timothy and Esther Stoddard Edwards in AD 1703.
      i. Timothy had attended and graduated from Harvard.

   ii. After graduating, Timothy, a Puritan, took the position of pastor in a church in East Windsor, Connecticut.
   iii. Edwards was the fifth of eleven children—the only boy.
B. Timothy ministered at the church in East Windsor for fifty-six years.
   i. Timothy's wife, Esther Stoddard, was the daughter of Solomon Stoddard, the pastor of First Congregational Church in Northampton, Massachusetts.
      1. Esther, like her sisters but unlike the general female populace, received education from her father at home in Latin, Greek, and Hebrew.
      2. She was sent to finishing school in Boston, and throughout her life she exhibited fine mental gifts and a strong personality.
      3. Timothy and Esther sent all of Jonathan's sisters to finishing school, and his older sisters participated in teaching him.
C. Jonathan witnessed the many dimensions of pastoral ministry as Timothy's son.
   i. On the one hand, Jonathan witnessed the church grow and learned the art of powerful preaching.
      1. The first letter extant from Jonathan describes a revival he witnessed in the church of his father.
      2. While in East Windsor, Jonathan learned how to preach in a school of preaching in the Connecticut River Valley.
         a. The Puritans considered preaching an art form.
         b. Sermons were designed to persuade by the power of words, arguments, and letting the Word of God go forth.
   ii. On the other hand, Jonathan saw the difficulties many pastors faced during this era.
      1. The church at East Windsor neglected to pay Timothy his wages, forcing him to supplement his income by serving as a chaplain for the British forces.
      2. Timothy's absence while serving as a chaplain demanded that Jonathan's sisters pick up his education.
   iii. During his youth, Edwards determined that a life that matters is the life lived for a singular, intentional purpose.
D. In 1716, at the age of twelve, Jonathan prepared to attend college.
   i. Although Timothy and much of his family attended Harvard, he decided against sending Jonathan there.
      1. Timothy, like many Puritans, suspected that Harvard had fallen into latitudinarianism.
         a. Many believed that Harvard provided too much latitude on adherence to the Westminster Confession of Faith.
         b. Whereas before, this confession undergirded Harvard, by the 1710's it had ceased to hold this sort of sway amongst the faculty and student body.

        2. A new college, largely in response to Harvard's theological movement, had opened in nearby New Haven, Connecticut—Yale.
    ii. Timothy sent Jonathan to Yale in 1716.
        1. Jonathan soon wrote home to his parents requesting more money to buy schoolbooks.
        2. As we will see throughout this series, Jonathan, a true Puritan, desired to study not only God's revelation in His Word but also His revelation in creation.

STUDY QUESTIONS

1. After graduating from Harvard, Timothy Edwards took a position as pastor in a church at ___________.
    a. Northampton, Massachusetts
    b. East Windsor, Connecticut
    c. Cambridge, Massachusetts
    d. New Haven, Connecticut

2. Esther Stoddard Edwards proved a hardworking housewife, but she came up short in the area of academics.
    a. True
    b. False

3. Jonathan witnessed the many dimensions of pastoral ministry while growing up in Timothy's household.
    a. True
    b. False

4. Puritan preaching employed gimmicks, tricks, and theatrics to move and sway the congregation.
    a. True
    b. False

5. At Timothy's discretion, Jonathan attended this school for his college education.
    a. The University of Pennsylvania
    b. Harvard University
    c. Yale University
    d. Oxford University

BIBLE STUDY AND DISCUSSION QUESTIONS

1. Describe how Jonathan's immediate and extended family valued education among all of its members. How did this affect Jonathan's own life, particularly in regards to his mother and sisters?

2. What are some of the positive experiences Jonathan had on account of Timothy's ministry in East Windsor?

3. What are some of the negative experiences Jonathan underwent on account of Timothy's ministry in East Windsor?

4. Why did Timothy send Jonathan to Yale instead of Harvard? Define "latitudinarianism," and explain its relevance in Timothy's decision.

5. On what principles was Yale founded? Does the school exemplify these principles today? Why or why not, and what does this trend say about many of the higher academic institutions in the United States?

6. What does Jonathan's letter to his parents requesting money for textbooks reveal about his attitude toward his studies?

2

A Minister of the Gospel

MESSAGE INTRODUCTION

At a young age—no later than nineteen—Jonathan Edwards sat down to write his resolutions. He would eventually produce seventy resolutions, a large number, to be sure. Yet, the penning of resolutions was not anomalous in Edwards' era. Benjamin Franklin, for instance, also composed his own list, although he limited his resolutions to thirteen. Educated men and women undertook this task to promote self-contemplation and the cultivation of character. The defining feature of Edwards' resolutions, however, involves the ability to keep them. Whereas most men, Franklin among them, followed the ideals of the Enlightenment, believing themselves masters of their own nature through reason, Edwards understood his sinful nature and placed himself humbly at the grace of God. Only by the goodness of His Creator could he hope to remain faithful to the resolutions. This Spirit-filled humility would serve him well throughout his time at Yale and during the early stages of his ministry.

TEACHING OBJECTIVES

1. To detail Edwards' time at Yale and the events that occurred during his studies
2. To demonstrate the intellectual capabilities, spiritual maturity, and altruism Edwards possessed even as a young man
3. To introduce and provide information on Edwards' marriage and family
4. To explain how Edwards arrived in Northampton and the original intention of his succession of Solomon Stoddard

QUOTATION

> *Resolved, that I will do whatsoever I think to be most to God's glory, and my own good, profit and pleasure, in the whole of my duration, without any consideration of the time, whether now, or never so many myriad's of ages hence. Resolved to do whatever I think to be my duty and most for the good and advantage of mankind in general. Resolved to do this, whatever difficulties I meet with, how many and how great soever.*
>
> —Jonathan Edwards, Resolution 1

LECTURE OUTLINE

I. Edwards at Yale
   A. Edwards completed a bachelor's and a master's degree while at Yale.
      i. Edwards produced his master's thesis entirely in Latin.
      ii. Edwards' thesis was a statement on justification by faith.
   B. While writing his master's thesis, Edwards took his first pastorate at a Presbyterian church in New York City.
      i. Although raised a Congregationalist, Edwards took the position of pastor over a splinter group off of a Presbyterian church at Broad and Wall Street.
      ii. Edwards pastored the church at the docks of the New York Harbor, and the location varied greatly from his hometown of East Windsor.
         1. Edwards was only nineteen years old.
         2. He was not used to the movement and size of the city.
   C. During his pastorate, Edwards wrote a series of resolutions to govern his life.
      i. The preface of the resolutions acknowledged his limitations and sinfulness, and in it he requested that God, in His grace, enable him to perform them.
      ii. Edwards resolved to live his life for the glory of God and in such a manner that would remove all regrets on his deathbed.
   D. After a short span of his pastorate, Edwards counseled the church to rejoin the church from which they split.
      i. Edwards' actions are remarkable for two reasons.
         1. They demonstrate his ability to deal with an older congregation at the age of nineteen.
         2. They demonstrate his altruism, for this move would lead to his unemployment.
      ii. Edwards' church rejoined its former congregation, and Edwards, unemployed, moved back to his parents house to finish his master's thesis.
   E. Edwards wrote a piece on the flying spider while studying at Yale.
      i. After observing the insect, Edwards analyzed and described its pattern of movement, noting that the spider did not fly but floated through the air—sometimes out to the Atlantic Ocean.

1. From his observations, Edwards determined that the spiders enjoyed their "flight."
2. Further, Edwards agreed that their misdirection to the ocean prevented the spiders from becoming too numerous.

ii. Edwards' piece, although never published, illuminates a number of aspects about his person.

1. Edwards possessed many interests, and he had a keen, analytical mind.
2. Most importantly, Edwards had a strong desire to witness how God, in His goodness, provides for the necessities and pleasures of all His creatures, great and small.

F. After completing his master's thesis, Edwards stayed at Yale and taught.

i. Samuel Johnson, the rector of Yale, converted to Anglicanism while Edwards was teaching.

1. Johnson's conversion was considered a great apostasy, and he left the college.
2. Edwards played a key role in sustaining the college during this difficult period.

ii. In 1727, Edwards met Sarah Pierpont, the daughter of John Pierpont, one of the founders of Yale.

1. Edwards was smitten with Sarah, particularly over her relationship with the Lord.
2. Nonetheless, Edwards, as an academic, was hindered in marrying Sarah on account of his financial prospects.

II. The Beginning of Edwards' Ministry in Northampton

A. In 1727, Edwards was invited to serve as the assistant minister to Solomon Stoddard, his grandfather, in Northampton, Massachusetts.

i. Solomon Stoddard held a powerful reputation in the Connecticut River Valley.

ii. As he approached the twilight of his life, the church wanted to pick his successor.

iii. In 1727, the Northampton Congregational Church ordained Edwards as the assistant minister to Stoddard.

B. Having attained a respectable and stable position, Edwards married Sarah Pierpont in the same year as his ordination.

i. Edwards and Sarah had eleven children.

ii. Although Edwards spent much of his time studying and was not very sociable, he held Sarah in very high regard.

C. Two years into his post as assistant pastor in Northampton, Stoddard passed away and left Edwards in charge of the second largest church in the colonies—as a twenty-six year old.

STUDY QUESTIONS

1. Edwards wrote and defended his master's thesis in Classical Hebrew.
    a. True
    b. False

2. While writing his master's thesis, Edwards took the position of pastor in a Presbyterian church in ___________.
    a. New York City
    b. Boston
    c. Providence
    d. New Haven

3. Edwards focused all of his academic attentions on theological and biblical studies, considering pursuit in the physical sciences unimportant.
    a. True
    b. False

4. Edwards accepted the role of assistant pastor in his father's church in East Windsor.
    a. True
    b. False

5. In 1727, Edwards married ___________, a daughter of one of the founders of Yale.
    a. Esther Burr
    b. Elizabeth Stoddard
    c. Hannah Smith
    d. Sarah Pierpont

BIBLE STUDY AND DISCUSSION QUESTIONS

1. Describe Edwards' first pastorate. What did his ministry there demonstrate about his character?

2. Why did Edwards write a series of resolutions while ministering in New York City? How did Edwards seek to complete the resolutions? How would you summarize the purpose of Edwards' resolutions?

3. What does Edwards' study of the flying spiders in New England demonstrate about his character? What are Edwards' conclusions, and why are they significant?

4. Describe the "great apostasy" of Samuel Johnson at Yale. What role did Edwards play at Yale during this time?

5. Why did the church in Northampton call Edwards to be assistant minister to Solomon Stoddard? What was their design for succession?

6. Describe Edwards' immediate family? How was his marriage to Sarah? How did he regard her?

3

The Great Awakening

MESSAGE INTRODUCTION

The Puritans are encumbered by a caricature of strictness and dourness in our day and age. Their mention calls forth images of judgment, wrath, and superstition, and almost without doubt people look to Jonathan Edwards' sermon "Sinners in the Hands of an Angry God" as the paradigm of this group's sentiment. Sadly, this caricature fails to do justice to Edwards and the Puritans, as it captures only a small part of the gospel they preached. Edwards and his Puritan contemporaries knew well the condemnation promised by God for disobedience, but they knew it in light of the great promise of salvation offered by the gospel. Edwards wrote more about the joy, pleasure, and happiness of salvation than anything else, and during the Great Awakening he poured out this message of grace that promises eternal life for undeserving sinners.

TEACHING OBJECTIVES

1. To explain many of the events occurring while Edwards ministered in Northampton
2. To describe the evolution of Edwards' sermon preparation and delivery
3. To chronicle many events leading to and occurring in the Great Awakening, as well as illuminating Edwards role in this revival

QUOTATION

And let every one that is yet out of Christ, and hanging over the pit of hell, whether they be old men and women, or middle aged, or young people, or little children, now hearken to the loud calls of God's word and providence. This acceptable year of the Lord, a day of such great favour to some, will doubtless be a day of as remarkable vengeance to others. Men's hearts harden, and their guilt increases apace at such a day as this, if they neglect their souls; and never was there so great danger of such persons being given up to hardness of heart and blindness of mind. God seems now to be hastily gathering in his elect in all parts of the land; and probably the greater part of adult persons that ever shall be saved, will be brought in now in a little time, and that it will be as it was on the great out-pouring of the Spirit upon the Jews in the apostles' days; the election will obtain, and the rest will be blinded. If this should be the case with you, you will eternally curse this day, and will curse the day that ever you was born, to see such a season of the pouring out of God's Spirit, and will wish that you had died and gone to hell before you had seen it. Now undoubtedly it is, as it was in the days of John the Baptist, the axe is in an extraordinary manner laid at the root of the trees, that every tree which brings not forth good fruit, may be hewn down and cast into the fire.

—From Jonathan Edwards' sermon, "Sinners in the Hands of an Angry God"

LECTURE OUTLINE

I. Edwards at Northampton
- A. Edwards began serving as the assistant minister at First Congregational Church of Northampton in 1729.
  - i. He served at the second largest congregation in the colonies, First Congregational Church in Boston being the largest.
  - ii. While pastoring at Northampton, Harvard invited Edwards to give its commencement address.
    1. Harvard bestowed a great honor on Edwards with this invitation, and commencement played an important role in the life of the city, the university, and among ministers formerly trained there.
    2. Edwards preached a sermon entitled "God Glorified in Man's Dependence."
       - a. The sermon stressed that salvation is from start to finish a work of God.
       - b. His sermon was well received and eventually published in conjunction with a sermon by William Williams—a decision that would affect Edwards later in his life.
- B. Edwards prepared his sermons with meticulous effort and care.
  - i. Edwards wrote roughly forty to sixty pages for each sermon.
    1. The entire sermon was most likely delivered in intervals.
    2. Although Edwards is commonly attributed with reading his manuscripts while presenting the sermon, he more likely memorized his sermons and delivered them from memory.
  - ii. When George Whitefield came to Northampton, Edwards changed the method of his sermon delivery.
    1. Whitefield was a great orator, and he delivered his sermons passionately and often times spontaneously.
    2. After witnessing Whitefield's example, Edwards no longer prepared his manuscript.
       - a. He took only an outline into the pulpit.

b. After the sermon, Edwards would go into his study and record the sermon he preached.

iii. It is estimated that Edwards preached between 1,200 to 1,400 sermons.

II. The Great Awakening

A. The Connecticut River Valley experienced a revival largely due to Edwards preaching between 1734 and 1735.

i. Edwards traveled up and down the valley preaching.

ii. Edwards wrote a description of the revival and sent it to the papers in Boston to encourage revival there.

1. Via an editor of a paper in Boston, the letter reached Isaac Watts in England, and he requested that Edwards write a fuller version for publication as a book.

a. In 1736, Edwards wrote *A Faithful Narrative of the Surprising Work of God in the Conversion of Many Hundred Souls in Northampton in the Neighboring Towns and Villages of Hampshire in New England.*

b. Watts committed many editorial errors in the work, not the least of which occurs in the title, which prompted Edwards to re-edit the book and send it for printing in Boston.

2. Many consider this work one of the seeds that would grow into the Great Awakening of 1740 to 1742.

B. The Great Awakening, a spiritual revival of great magnitude, occurred both in England and the United States between the years of 1740 and 1742.

i. In England, George Whitefield and John and Charles Wesley led many to Christ.

1. Whitefield and the Wesley brothers confronted the nominal Christianity present in the Anglican Church, the state church of England.

2. The Anglican Church refused to open their doors to these preachers, so they preached outside.

3. Their efforts saw many come to Christ, particularly in Newcastle.

ii. Whitefield eventually traveled to America to preach, where he began an orphanage in Georgia and proceeded to preach through the colonies.

1. The revival quickly caught on in the United States.

2. Even people like Benjamin Franklin, a noted deist, were influenced by the powerful preaching of Whitefield.

C. The Great Awakening had advocates and detractors.

i. Detractors denied the legitimacy of revivals (e.g. Charles Chauncy).

ii. Advocates believed the Holy Spirit was at work behind the revival, with some taking drastic measures to prove this point (e.g. James Davenport).

D. Some believe the Great Awakening contributed to the American Revolution in the late eighteenth century.

i. The creation of newspapers to communicate revival news assisted in increasing awareness about current events.

ii. The Great Awakening provided a sense of unity amongst individual colonies with individual identities.

E. Edwards sat right in the middle of the Great Awakening.

i. Edwards preached and played a pivotal role in this revival, and his sermon "Sinners in the Hands of an Angry God" remains the most well known sermon in American history.

ii. The sermon expresses judgment for a failure to repent, but it also expresses the joy and beauty of salvation found through Christ—a theme that characterized Edwards preaching and ministry.

STUDY QUESTIONS

1. While ministering in Northampton, Edwards was invited to give the commencement address at __________.
   a. the University of Pennsylvania
   b. Yale University
   c. Reformed Theological Seminary
   d. Harvard University

2. Edwards was so gifted that he never prepared for his sermons and spontaneously delivered them on every occasion.
   a. True
   b. False

3. George Whitefield and Jonathan Edwards had a fierce, even hostile, rivalry.
   a. True
   b. False

4. George Whitefield and John and Charles Wesley were unsuccessful in bringing revival to England, so they traveled to the United States.
   a. True
   b. False

5. What is Edwards' most famous sermon?
   a. "A Faithful Narrative of the Surprising Work of God"
   b. "On the Soul"
   c. "Religious Affections"
   d. "Sinners in the Hands of an Angry God"

BIBLE STUDY AND DISCUSSION QUESTIONS

1. Why was Harvard's offer to deliver a commencement speech such an honor for Edwards? What did his sermon, "God Glorified in Man's Dependence," emphasize?

2. Describe Edwards' sermon preparation prior to 1741. How did Whitefield's visit to Northampton affect Edwards' sermon preparation?

3. Explain how Edward's book *A Faithful Narrative of the Surprising Work of God in the Conversion of Many Hundred Souls in Northampton in the Neighboring Towns and Villages of Hampshire in New England* came into existence. What impact did this book have on the colonies?

4. Who were some of the key figures in the Great Awakening of England and the United States in the eighteenth century? How did the revival proceed in England?

5. How did the Great Awakening contribute to the American Revolution?

6. How are the Puritans caricatured in our day and age? Does Edwards' sermon "Sinners in the Hands of an Angry God" defy or support this caricature? Explain.

4

His Big Idea

MESSAGE INTRODUCTION

Jonathan Edwards is often portrayed as a disgruntled, unhappy figure concerned only about judgment and doom. With titles for his works such as *Original Sin* and "Sinners in the Hands of an Angry God," what more should we expect? As a matter of fact, the opposite is true of Edwards. We would be hard pressed to find another theologian so full of joy, so delighted in the goodness and bountiful provision of His Lord. Edwards was enraptured with the beauty and wonder of God's blessings, and he relished the sweetness of God's greatest gift to His people: Himself. Edwards understood that man's greatest pleasure rested in the glorification of God and the enjoyment of Him.

TEACHING OBJECTIVES

1. To describe many of Edwards' influential works and the circumstances contributing to their composition
2. To detail some of Edwards' idiosyncrasies in order to shed light on his life and works
3. To find in Edwards' works the major theme that defined his life and doctrine

QUOTATION

After this, my sense of divine things gradually increased, and became more and more lively, and had more of that inward sweetness. The appearance of everything was altered. There seemed to be, as it were, a calm, sweet cast or appearance of divine glory in almost everything. God's excellency, His wisdom, His purity, and love seemed to appear in everything; in the sun, moon, and stars; in the clouds and the blue sky; in the grass, flowers, and trees; in the water and all nature which used greatly to fix my mind.

—An excerpt from Edwards' *The Personal Narrative*

LECTURE OUTLINE

I. The Works of Edwards
   A. In the sermon he preached in 1731 for Harvard's commencement, "God Glorified in Man's Dependence," Edwards proclaimed that when the Holy Spirit works salvation in the heart, God proceeds to give the regenerate believer wonderful gifts.
      i. The full title of the sermon is "God Glorified in the Work of Redemption As Seen in Man's Dependence on Him."
      ii. Edwards preached that when God saves people, He gives them wonderful gifts, the foremost being the gift of Himself.
         1. God provides believers with the highest good: Himself.
         2. Not only does God provide Himself as a possession, He desires that the redeemed enjoy Him.
   B. In 1734, Edwards wrote the story of his own conversion in the work he titled *The Personal Narrative.*
      i. Aaron Burr Sr., Edwards' son-in-law and a founder and second president of Princeton University, requested that Edwards write a narrative of his conversion for the benefit of the young men at Princeton.
      ii. In *The Personal Narrative*, Edwards chronicled his conversion and the subsequent "sweetness" he experienced as a redeemed son of God.
         1. Edwards wrote that he "relished" God.
         2. Edwards understood well that the chief end of man is to glorify God and to enjoy Him forever, and he made this truth the center of his life and theology.
   C. Edwards possessed a number of idiosyncratic tendencies in formulating his thoughts and recording them.
      i. Edwards enjoyed physical activity, and he believed everybody should engage in it for their health.
         1. Edwards rode on horseback through the Connecticut River Valley as a part of his physical exertion.
         2. During his rides, Edward would pin pieces of cloth to his jacket as he formulated thoughts on specific topics.
            a. He associated each piece of cloth with a specific thought.
            b. When he returned from riding, Edwards would inscribe his thoughts. He called these writings "miscellanies."
            c. Edwards produced more than fifteen hundred of these miscellanies, and he used intricate filing systems to record and hold them.
      ii. Edwards wrote his works on almost any form of paper he found, including between the lines of books written in French.
      iii. Edwards' ideas, recorded in his miscellanies and the blank pages of the special Bible his brother-in-law gave to him, eventually found their way into his sermons, which fed into his treaties.
         1. Edwards' work *Religious Affections*, published in 1746, represents a perfect example of this process.

a. Edwards recorded his thoughts concerning revivalism during the Great Awakening.
b. Later, Edwards wrote a series of sermons from his thoughts, exploring the question of revivals and other issues associated with it.
c. The book *Religious Affections* sprang from his sermons.

2. Edwards duplicated this task in his work *History of the Work of Redemption.*
   a. The Puritans employed a sermon model that consisted of the presentation of the text, followed by the exposition of doctrine, and concluded with application (also called the "use" or the "improvement").
   b. Edwards applied this model to half a verse of Isaiah 51:8, creating thirty sermons that he later converted into *History of the Work of Redemption.*

D. In the 1750s, near the end of his life, Edwards wrote a number of important treatises.
   i. These treatises include *Freedom of the Will, Original Sin,* and what has come to be called "The Two Dissertations."
   ii. The second of two dissertations, titled *The End For Which God Created the World* and published posthumously in 1759, summarized the main theme running through all of Edwards' works.
      1. Edwards concluded that all things, great and small, are created by God for His glory.
      2. When man lives for this glory, he receives his greatest enjoyment and sense of purpose.

STUDY QUESTIONS

1. In his sermon "God Glorified in Man's Dependence," Edwards concludes that the highest good is ___________.
   a. family
   b. creation
   c. God
   d. marriage

2. Edwards confessed in *The Personal Narrative* that, as a Christian, he had to work very hard to find delight and joy in God's creation.
   a. True
   b. False

3. Edwards formed his sermons from the lengthy books he produced, after which he categorized the thoughts of his sermons into "miscellanies."
   a. True
   b. False

4. The *History of the Work of Redemption* was formed by thirty sermons on a half of a verse in the book of Isaiah.
   a. True
   b. False

5. What treatise did Edwards write near the end of his life that captured the central theme running through his life and works?
   a. *Original Sin*
   b. *Freedom of the Will*
   c. *The Institutes of the Christian Religion*
   d. *The End For Which God Created the World*

BIBLE STUDY AND DISCUSSION QUESTIONS

1. What was the main point of Edwards' sermon "God Glorified in Man's Dependence"?

2. Why did Edwards write *The Personal Narrative*? What does the work reveal about his character and his theology?

3. How did Edwards remember his thoughts while riding through the country on horseback? Describe Edwards' system of recording his thoughts and categorizing them? What do his actions disclose about his mind?

4. Explain the process Edwards used that culminated in the writing of treatises. How did the Puritan model of sermon structure assist in this process?

5. Summarize the thesis of Edwards' work *The End For Which God Created the World*. When does this thesis reveal itself in the life of Edwards?

5

The Conflict at Northampton

MESSAGE INTRODUCTION

Jonathan Edwards was no stranger to controversy. Although admired and cherished around the globe for his preaching and contribution to the Great Awakening, his own congregation in Northampton, Massachusetts, opposed and removed him from the pulpit unjustly. Many men would have succumbed to bitterness over the controversy in which Edwards was embroiled, but he demonstrated his love for the Lord and His people by agreeing to preach at this same congregation while they searched for a new minister. Edwards desired that the love of God flowing forth from Him and filling heaven would burst forth onto the earth, even into the church that treated him so poorly. He desired that all men might know the goodness and love of God, and he left Northampton, not for a safe, comfortable pulpit in a large church, but for a missionary colony in the frontier.

TEACHING OBJECTIVES

1. To explain the events leading to Edwards' dismissal from Northampton
2. To describe why and how Edwards came to minister in the missionary colony of Stockbridge, Massachusetts

QUOTATION

The cause and fountain of love in heaven is in that the God of love Himself dwells in heaven. Heaven is the palace or presence-chamber of the high and holy One, whose name is love, and who is both the cause and source of all holy love. God, considered with respect to His essence, is everywhere—He fills both heaven and earth. But yet He is said, in some respects, to be more especially in some places than in others. He was said of old to dwell in the land of Israel, above all other lands; and in Jerusalem, above all other cities of that land; and in the temple, above all other buildings in the city; and in the holy of holies, above all other apartments of the temple; and on the mercy seat, over the ark of the covenant, above all other places in the holy of holies. But heaven is His dwelling-place above all other places in the universe; and all those places in which He was said to dwell of old, were but types of this. Heaven is a part of creation that God has built for this end, to be the place of His glorious presence, and it is His abode forever; and here will He dwell, and gloriously manifest Himself to all eternity.

—An excerpt from Edwards' sermon "Charity and Its Fruits"

LECTURE OUTLINE

I. Conflict at Northampton
  A. In the late 1740s, the fervor of the Great Awakening began to fade in Northampton.
  B. In 1746, Edwards challenged an institution of the church initiated by Edwards' predecessor and grandfather, Solomon Stoddard.
    i. The church of Northampton practiced a "halfway covenant," in which non-professing, baptized congregants could have their children baptized.
    ii. Stoddard applied this same principle to the Lord's Supper, extending the table to baptized, non-professing members of the church. (Stoddard understood the Lord's Supper as a converting ordinance.)
    iii. Edwards believed this practice was contributing to the spiritual laxity of the church, and he challenged it in order to stop people from drifting away from the gospel.
    iv. Edwards' efforts were met with resistance.
      1. The "old guard," those entrenched, older members dating back to Stoddard's era, opposed Edwards.
      2. The Williams family, still holding a bit of a grudge over the fact that William Williams, their relative, shared publication with the much younger Edwards, led this opposition.
      3. The event embroiled Edwards in controversy.
  C. In addition to the controversy of the halfway covenant, Edwards was caught up in a scandal concerning many young men in the church.
    i. Some of the young men had acquired a midwife's manual, and they were using it to harass the young women of the church.
    ii. Edwards named these young men from the pulpit, along with the witnesses of their indiscretion, creating animosity between the families of the culprits and him.
  D. Edwards' decision not to cultivate relationships while in Northampton but to focus on his gifts of preaching and teaching hindered him in raising support during this controversy.
  E. On June 22, 1750, the First Congregational Church of Northampton dismissed Edwards from his position as pastor.

i. Edwards requested that his case be turned over to the synod of ministers that presided over the churches in Hampshire.
   1. The synod consisted largely of ministers from the Williams family.
   2. In a close vote, with many of Edwards' supporters unable to arrive to the meeting in time, the synod upheld the decision.

ii. At the congregation's request, Edward agreed to stay on and preach for the church until they found another minister, and he even refused to begin another in Northampton with eager members.

II. The Decision to Move to Stockbridge, Massachusetts
   A. Edwards received many offers for a pastoral position, with enquiries coming as far as Scotland, but he declined.
   B. Edwards possessed a strong heart for missions, and he desired to see the gospel spread to the Native Americans living in Stockbridge.
      i. Stockbridge was founded as a missionary colony to the Mohicans in 1739.
         1. The Mohicans permanently resided in this location.
         2. A Williams' relative, the widow of the founding pastor spurned by one of Edwards' sisters, resided in the colony and would eventually cause trouble for Edwards.
      ii. Edwards always had a strong desire to serve as a missionary to the Native Americans, and his dismissal from the congregation in Northampton opened up this opportunity.
   C. While Edwards was engaged in controversy in Northampton, Edwards preached a sermon from 1 Corinthians 13, which he called "Charity and Its Fruits."
      i. Edward declared that the "Triune God exists in perfect and total harmony and love," and "if heaven is a world of love, then the way to heaven is the way of love."
      ii. Even amidst controversy, Edwards still longed for his congregation to imitate this vision of love and harmony.

STUDY QUESTIONS

1. Solomon Stoddard vehemently fought against the halfway covenant, but the old guard opposed him successfully.
   a. True
   b. False

2. Edwards met the most resistance while at Northampton from the __________.
   a. Williams family
   b. Mather family
   c. Washington family
   d. Whitefield family

3. Edwards cultivated many personal relationships in Northampton that worked in his favor when controversy embroiled him.
   a. True
   b. False

4. Edwards' case was overturned in his favor, but he decided to leave the church for the good of the congregation.
   a. True
   b. False

5. Which tribe of Native Americans inhabited Stockbridge?
   a. Iroquois
   b. Mohican
   c. Navajo
   d. Apache

BIBLE STUDY AND DISCUSSION QUESTIONS

1. Explain the halfway covenant in First Congregational Church of Northampton. How did Stoddard view the position? Why did Edwards challenge it? Who opposed him and why?

2. What other controversy beside the halfway covenant embroiled Edwards? How did Edwards upset some of the congregants in this situation?

3. What might Edwards have done differently while pastoring in Northampton? How did Edwards' pastoral decisions affect him when controversy arrived?

4. Why did Edwards accept the offer to pastor in Stockbridge?

5. Summarize Edwards' sermon "Charity and Its Fruits." When did Edwards deliver this sermon, and what does it tell us about his character?

6

The Missionary

MESSAGE INTRODUCTION

Jonathan Edwards died at the age of fifty-five. Although not young, relative to our era it seems premature. What might his mind have produced if he possessed even a few more years on this earth? Edwards would probably have never entertained this thread of thought. He understood that God's providence never fails to accomplish its task perfectly and to completion. God had other plans for Edwards, and none of them went awry. On the contrary, He demonstrated his faithfulness to this man and his family despite the tragic conditions under which they died. He brought them home to heaven, where they reside in the love of our Savior.

TEACHING OBJECTIVES

1. To detail the Edwards' time at Stockbridge and the lasting effects they produced on the missionary colony
2. To explain the events leading to the Edwards' departure to Princeton
3. To chronicle Jonathan's death
4. To illustrate Edwards' view of providence

QUOTATION

God's providence may not unfitly be compared to a large and long river, having innumerable branches, beginning in different regions, and at a great distance one from another, and all conspiring to one common issue. After their very diverse and apparent contrary courses, they all collect together, the nearer they come to their common end, and at length discharge themselves at one mouth into the same ocean. Not one of the streams shall fail.

—An excerpt from Edwards' *History of the Work of Redemption*

LECTURE OUTLINE

I. The Edwards at Stockbridge
   A. The Edwards family became engaged in all elements of life when they moved to the missionary colony of Stockbridge.
      i. Hendrick Aupaumut, a Mohican hero of the Seven Years War upon which James Fennimore Cooper based his novel *Last of the Mohicans*, became friends with Timothy Edwards, Jonathan's son.
         1. Timothy stayed in Stockbridge after his father's passing, and Aupaumut requested Jonathan's works from Timothy in order to read them.
         2. Aupaumut also translated the Westminster Shorter Catechism into Mohican.
         3. This demonstrates the impact the Edwards family had in Stockbridge.
      ii. Jonathan Edwards Jr. wrote a Mohican grammar.
      iii. Edwards preached the gospel faithfully in Stockbridge, but he also pursued social justice for the Mohicans.
         1. Edwards consistently wrote the governor of Massachusetts over civil infractions by the colonists against the Mohicans.
         2. Edwards was invited to preach at the signing of a peace treaty.
            a. The gathering consisted of colonial and Native American dignitaries.
            b. Edwards apologized for the failure of the colonists to treat the Native Americans properly.
   B. Edwards spent a good deal of his time at Stockbridge writing.
      i. Some scholars argue that Edwards treated his tenure at Stockbridge as a sabbatical.
         1. Edwards spent much of his time writing treatises, including *Freedom of the Will* and *Original Sin*.
         2. He did not need to preach or prepare sermons in the same manner as in Northampton.
      ii. While Edwards did write more, the demands of Stockbridge accounted for his schedule, not a sabbatical.
         1. The congregation of Stockbridge was reduced by two-thirds.
         2. Edwards, similar to most pastors, reworked and recycled his sermons in this new location.
         3. Edwards probably engaged more in church life than he ever did in Northampton.
   C. During Edwards' tenure in Stockbridge, his son-in-law and the president of Princeton University, Aaron Burr Sr., died.
      i. The trustees wrote to Edwards offering him the position of president.
      ii. Edwards wanted to decline, but he submitted the request to a synod of ministers, who agreed that he should leave Stockbridge and take the post.
      iii. In 1758, Edwards, with a heavy heart, left Stockbridge for New Jersey.

II. The Edwards at Princeton
   A. Edwards traveled to Princeton by himself while Sarah stayed behind to close their affairs in Stockbridge.
   B. Edwards was installed as president in February of 1758.
   C. Almost immediately following his induction, Edwards received a small pox vaccination to encourage the students to do the same.
      i. Edwards reacted poorly to the vaccination and died of dehydration on March 22 of the same year.
      ii. Esther Edwards Burr, Jonathan's widowed daughter, died of complications from the small pox vaccination that same month.
      iii. Sarah, who traveled to Philadelphia to raise Esther's children, died shortly after of dysentery.
   D. Edwards' death may seem untimely, but the last sermon from his series *History of the Work of Redemption* demonstrates that his death occurred in the perfect timing of our Redeemer.
      i. Edwards compared God's providence to a river possessing many branches, curves, and obstacles.
         1. If we possessed a bird's eye view of this river, we would likely be fearful and overcome by all the obstacles.
         2. However, all the streams reach the ocean, and none of them fail.
      ii. Edwards understood that God's will is always done, and His promise to remain faithful to all generations of those who love Him will never fail, no matter what it might look like from our perspective.

STUDY QUESTIONS

1. Hendrick Aupaumut's translation of the Westminster Shorter Catechism demonstrates the lasting effect the Edwards made on Stockbridge.
   a. True
   b. False

2. Jonathan Edwards Jr. wrote a ___________.
   a. treaty on the souls of animals
   b. book of poems about the Adirondack Mountains
   c. Mohican grammar
   d. novel, titled *Last of the Mohicans*

3. Edwards cared very much that the Native Americans received civil justice.
   a. True
   b. False

4. Edwards accepted the position of president at what university?
   a. Harvard
   b. Yale
   c. Pennsylvania
   d. Princeton

5. Edwards died of complications from a small pox vaccination within months of his installment as president of the university.
   a. True
   b. False

BIBLE STUDY AND DISCUSSION QUESTIONS

1. List pieces of evidence showing that the Edwards contributed greatly to the missionary colony at Stockbridge.

2. How were the Native Americans, particularly the Mohicans, being abused during Edwards' era? Did Edwards care? If yes, what did he do to remedy the problem?

3. Why is Edwards' time in Stockbridge often referred to as a sabbatical? Why is this an incorrect assessment?

4. How did the position of president at Princeton become available? Did Edwards want to take the position? Why or why not? What convinced him to go to Princeton?

5. How and when did Edwards die? Is Edwards' death untimely? How would Edwards answer this? How did Edwards understand providence to work?